PRAISE FOR *INTO THE ETHER*

"Kate Bank's poetry revels in the exquisite essence of everyday things and the spirituality of the undiscovered. *Into the Ether* is a journey into the elusive and the incarnate, into self, and into the margins. Each poem builds a history, layered like sediment, of a life of observations, of tragedy, of connection, with one inevitable conclusion. Kate's calm tone and vivid imagery remind us that we all have time to grow, to appreciate, to see, and ultimately, chart our own course into the ether. These are works you'll surely return to again and again."

—JW McAteer, publisher, *Etched Onyx Magazine*

"How tempting it is to describe the poetry of *Into the Ether* as breathtaking. Tempting…but completely off the mark. The usual descriptors simply don't capture the beautiful and brutal vitalities of Bank's opusI where shes holds the purity of paradox in a resolute embrace. She finds home in the thin places, the forests where the thin veil between the familiar world and the 'other' world offers us a glimpse of the sacred seam where 'silence is distilled from a hundred sounds' and life and death collide. It is from these locations that pinecones swim upstream and become fish; where wounds, trauma, and broken souls are an alchemy that produces 'the gold of human existence.' Similarly, Bank's intimacy with the natural world is expressed through reverence. Never does her poetry devolve into prettification. The gorgeous pink blossoms of 'Oleanders' standing guard on the sacred seam of road and turf with their long, tapered leaves might just as surely be poisoned pistols. She mourns the shredded remains of a bird, the mountain boulders that fell trees and demolish the perfect world of sandcastles and mudpies. Yet she senses that all is holy and ephemeral, from the grand sanctuaries of ancient Rome to the mounds of dog shit on the sidewalk. Throughout Banks offers us a glimpse into the world where she is a part of all, but attached to nothing; where many become one, and one becomes many. She invites the reader to savor the scanty moments of stillness and to befriend death, knowing that death is another beginning. *Into the Ether* is a summons to journey with her Soul Body and an invitation to embrace our own, if only we dare."

—Dr. Maureen Walker, licensed clinical psychologist, author of *When Getting Along is Not Enough: Reconstructing Race in our Lives and Relationships*

"Kate Banks brings beauty to life in moments of simple remembrance. She invites the reader to walk with her as she finds joy and is touched by pain. Her images are blessings.....stunning. Her love goes straight to the heart. The words are gentle, clear, breath-giving, breath-taking, heart-warming and heart-breaking. My tears speak my gratitude. Thank you, Kate."

—Judith V. Jordan PhD, associate professor Harvard Medical School, Founding Scholar Relational-Cultural Theory

"CS Lewis suggested we read to know we are not alone. In poetry, I would add, we read to feel that even in our aloneness, we belong. Kate Bank's poetry gently dares us to stare into the sun of our shared humanity—bravely refusing to blink whether we're seeing into the 'cracks of eternity,' 'beguiled by the beauty' of ancient timber, or refusing to 'burn the roots' of our beloveds. Kate embraces the burden of being poetically sourced by the Muses with diligent grace, recanting stories of the mystical landscapes of her youth and her lived mysteries thereafter as only a 'scribe of the Celestial Soup' could master. Her poems are a literary Cirque du Soleil—words and metaphors trapeze artists on the page. So aptly titled, *Into the Ether* is as gripping and grounding as it is transcendent. Read it to be reminded you are not alone and you belong."

—Beth Hartman McGilley, PhD, FAED, CEDS-S

licensed clinical psychologist fellow, Academy for Eating Disorders certified eating disorders specialist/supervisor

"Kate Banks's poetry infuses me with the sense that literally everything is alive! Plants twist and climb, insects protest, clouds nourish, branches make wishes, the wind turns over in its sleep, the seasons know where to find us, stones weather the drub of footsteps and in soup support our bones, chairs are waiting with arms spread wide, mountains buck boulders, olive trees rouse the pines and sycamores and know things we don't, the equator tightens its belt, when the moon speaks 'wolf' you can hear the voice of God, emptiness gives birth, stillness grieves, what has not yet happened is vibrant, the gold of humanity is found on the margins of society, death is another beginning, even a bullet leads to seeing God everywhere. In her poem saints and mystics, Banks writes: 'I have become accustomed to their vapors lingering in my space... They move through my life like others, infusing me with hope and strength.' In Kate I found a companion. I could not stop moving with her from poem to poem taking in the vapors, feeling myself lifted and then noticing the world around me become more vivid and alive!"

—William Larkin, faith leader, the Massachusetts Poor People's Campaign.

INTO THE ETHER

Kate Banks

Regal House Publishing

Published by
Regal House Publishing, LLC
Raleigh, NC 27605
All rights reserved

ISBN -13 (paperback): 9781646035267
ISBN -13 (epub): 9781646035274
Library of Congress Control Number:

All efforts were made to determine the copyright holders and obtain their permissions in any circumstance where copyrighted material was used. The publisher apologizes if any errors were made during this process, or if any omissions occurred. If noted, please contact the publisher and all efforts will be made to incorporate permissions in future editions.

Cover images and design by © C. B. Royal

Regal House Publishing, LLC
https://regalhousepublishing.com

The poems Still, The Noble Fig Tree, The Fallow Fields, Spring Cleaning, and Stone Soup first appeared in the Fall 2021 edition of *Etched Onyx Magazine*.

Printed in the United States of America

To Family

CONTENTS

Forward 1

1. THE OLIVE COTTAGE

The Olive Cottage 9

Family 11

The Bed on the Porch 13

Where the Bullfrogs Croak 15

All That Wildness 16

The Way of Worms 18

A Corn Kind of Day 19

A Lobster Kind of Day 21

That Kind of Woman 22

Waders and Flags 24

Heat Wave 27

By the Pond 28

The Fairy Queen 29

Someone 31

2. THE ROAD TO ROME

The Road to Rome 35

The Agony of Newness 38

How Different We Are 40

Plinktology 42

I Thought I Knew Old 44

Laundry 46

Holy 47

I Saw It in the Movies 48

The Thing About Wishes 49

Catacombs 51

Via Adda 52

About Clay. 53

Child of Fire 55

The Things We Tell Ourselves 56

How We Made Books 58

Bargaining 60

Friends of the Heart 62

Moving On 64

3. LA MAISON DES REVES

My House 69

Stone Soup. 72

Palm Trees 74

The Rebellion 76

Wisteria 78

Footstones 79

Once. 81

Milly Moon-face 83

Daybreak 85

Still 86

April. 88

The Noble Fig Tree. 90

We Lied 92

Murmuration 94

If Wishes Were Horses. 95

Spring Cleaning 96

Ascension. 98

The Fallow Fields 100

Devotion 102

Trespassers. 104

Sightseeing. 106

This Changing World 108

Come One, Come All 110

4. CONTEMPLATING COSMOS

Wheatgrass. 115

Living in the Margins 116

The Ecstasy of Treetops. 118

To Be a Star. 119

Just a Scribe. 121

Wolf Moon 122

Clouds 124

From Where I Sit 125

Shoring Up 127

5. INTO THE ETHER

Grief 131

What He did To Me 133

The Afterlife 135

The Place of Body Selection 137

Lemons and Leaves. 139

Rare Bird 140

Into the Ether 142

Practicing Death 144

Burn Baby Burn 145

Saints and Mystics. 146

Footsteps. 147

Why I Said No. 148

What do I Leave Them. 150

FOREWARD

AMY BANKS MD

Writing a foreward for my sister Kate's first poetry book is an honor, a privilege, and a far more difficult task than I had originally imagined. The challenge is not in knowing who Kate is or what I want to share about her and her work, but, rather, how to find words to describe this ethereal being who has embraced all life has thrown at her, the good, the bad and the ugly, knowing each experience, each moment is both a routine event and an exquisite part of the cadence of the universe.

Kate has always lived a life more complicated and nuanced than what appears on the surface and *Into the Ether* provides a window into this complexity. I have often marveled at how people respond to my description of my sister's seemingly idyllic life—the marriage to an Italian man and subsequent relocation to Rome where she became a mother to two beloved boys and a prolific and celebrated children's book author. When she and Pier moved the family to the south of France, Kate filled her days writing in her cozy study in Villa Bois Joli, tending to the boys and garden—her bounty she called it—and absorbing the wonders of the natural world around her. It is easy to mistake the scaffolding as evidence of a romantic, carefree life that many envied. The hard stuff was just below the surface—our father's murder her first year of college, a debilitating, misunderstood illness, and a botched medical treatment that left her in excruciating pain for years and drove her to master numerous non-traditional healing practices in order to heal herself.

After his death in 1979, our father was eulogized as a man with a vast expanse of knowledge, a professor of history who could ponder the great philosophers with the same passion and interest he brought to his research into local matters of his beloved state of Maine. Kate inherited his intellectual range with the ability to "contemplate the cosmos" as easily as she embraces the magic of an army of ants marching across her wall. This collection of poetry tells the story of pivotal periods in her life, transitions or moves that have shaped and broadened her ability to see the world around her through a unique lens. The noble fig tree, the swaying palm, the lizards, frogs, and other creatures she encounters are not foreign or other, but rather her friends and companions along her unique life's journey. Kate's descriptions of the natural world left me longing to meet the dogwood, coyotes and neighborhood cats living right outside my own door.

Born and raised in Maine, Kate grew up surrounded by nature and it has been a refuge for her when life delivered many sharp blows. Kate always understood that she is not only around nature but of nature, seeming to intuit the unity of the universe from a very young age. One of the ironies of Kate's life is the way she captures and conveys the essence of a mother's protective love for her children, despite the fact that she didn't have that in her own life. Her picture books describe the world to a child without masking its dangers and complexities, but always with a gentle, attentive parent guiding the way to help young children understand that what they are experiencing around them also lives in them. Her words deliver the most powerful message to a child—you belong, and you will be okay. As a psychiatrist specializing in trauma, I often share Kate's books with clients as a way of introducing them to the healing power of healthy, nurturing relationships.

The Olive Cottage, the setting of the first group of poems, was my family's summer place in Lincolnville, Maine, a forty-five minute drive from our home. Come June, our family would pile into the car with Kate and I singing "Leaving on a Jet Plane" in the back seat to pass the time. Weekends often started with Kate and I joining my father on his trips to Camden to buy a newspaper, secure fresh water to bring back to the cottage,

2

and to sit on the wharf in the harbor drinking rocket lemonade and eating Camden-bakery donuts. These remain some of my fondest childhood memories.

I always sensed that Kate possessed a 'knowing' but I didn't always understand how that worked. Even as a child she was a bit mysterious—the way she could escape into a book, her ability to excel in school and to hold onto her opinions and needs despite others telling her what they thought. Kate has always been the wisest, smartest person I know. And I suspect she was born that way. But her wisdom was further honed through her travels—emotionally and physically. She became an insightful and natural healer—the impetus to study non-traditional practices coming from her own need to heal and from the limitations of the western medical establishment. As a doctor, I can honestly say, her knowledge of the human body, how it works, and what it is capable of far exceeds that of any medical colleague I know. She heals by calling on energies and spirits beyond the human realm and trusts that they will be there. And more often than not, they are.

Through the years, I have witnessed Kate's creative process and it is as stunning as it is clear. When Kate moved to Rome in her twenties and started her own family, I loved visiting them all. Inevitably, as we walked down a street or through a park, she would get a far off look in her eyes and then suddenly come up with a book idea. Nine times out of ten, the book would be written in short order and published within a couple of years—it was clockwork. Her belief that she is simply a scribe (shared in the poem Only a Scribe), downloading messages from the universe, is hard to refute when reading the depth and wisdom of her words.

Kate often talks about her writing as being a process of channeling, but there's no doubt that extends to most everything she does. She simply lives on a different wavelength than most. For Kate to live is to create and she remains true to that motto. Her hands are a marvel with long slim fingers always in motion. Her creations are legendary—painting exquisitely detailed Ukrainian eggs, knitting a hat with a small wool version of her mini cooper sitting on top, building extravagant gingerbread houses with her boys every Christmas, whipping up a pair of sleep shorts in thirty minutes.

Though many reviews have described Kate's children's books as poetic, she began writing poetry seriously just a couple of years ago during the worst of the pandemic. It was a time when I was also going through some serious health issues. I was sick, vulnerable, and scared, and her poems tethered me to the natural world and reminded me that the energy of the universe holds the power to heal and that could be harnessed by the "all-knowing" body. She regularly sent me energy treatments from afar and I could feel them working in real time. She had tuned into a life force that could heal spontaneously if only we could get out of the way.

Her poetry has been a gift to me as the world has gotten crazier and crazier. What I gain in reading her gracious words grounds me to something bigger than human dominance and power. It also allows me to see Kate more clearly—she literally comes into high relief. She is a person of nature—it is what she trusts—not the icons that are thrown at us so casually —the doctors, the learned men and women. She listens to the universe—and though that spark was there always—it blossomed as she battled one health crisis after another. To Kate, her body was always a temporary weigh station for her soul, not in an abstract way to fend off the anxieties of living in such a harsh and intricate world, but because she could feel the energy of the universe just as easily as I felt and saw the concrete world around me.

This volume ends with a poem, What Will I Leave Them. Perhaps *Into the Ether* is what she will leave us all—her wisdom and way wrapped in a collection of poetry that shares what she sees when she looks out of her deep-set blue eyes. If you dare let the words sink in you may find a roadmap for how to live a life filled with vulnerability, courage, and grace. Kate's words have the power to break your heart wide open but at the same time ground you to the universe and all its wonder. To me, it is the emotional antidote to the tragic, chaotic, and fragmented world we are living in. Enjoy the dive.

1

THE OLIVE COTTAGE

THE OLIVE COTTAGE

They're at it again,
those carpenter ants,
snug kernels strung on mighty frames,
black as tar, gnawing at the beams,
guzzling sawdust,
much the same way that my
grandfather guzzled spirits.
He built the cottage,
bare hands, pine boards, and brew.
And he painted it olive green with white trim.
He built it for life, not death.

But what can I do?
Those damn ants and their grinding gears
that sound in my head,
even when I'm not there.

I wonder,
how long will it take for them to consume the cottage?
Will it collapse one day when I'm going about the business
of pondering the blueberry rake on the wall,
the torpid hinge on the screen door,
the pitiful shavings of pine scented soap
that cling to the porcelain sink,
all those things that tweak my senses?

Sometimes I'd like to spray the ants to kingdom come,
but I'm so used to their gnawing.
How could I manage without it,
or them?
If we could only find their nest.
But what then?

FAMILY

I remember,
back when I was seven,
I lay in the field
behind the Olive Cottage,
my spine pressed into the earth's bed.

I hid among the Queen Anne's lace,
platters of snowflakes
served up from the soul of Mother Earth,
the plucky brown-eyed susans with
their grainy gumdrop centers,
and the spiky stalks of grass.

The sky was a confounding blue,
never ending,
a blue I couldn't find elsewhere,
in anything.

In the distance I heard my brother's squeals.
He was capturing blood suckers,
dropping them into a metal pail
and shooting them with his BB gun,
hard round pellets that bruised my heart from afar.

And there was my mother's high-pitched laughter
that choked the silence,
my father, sitting in the lawn chair,
legs crossed, reading.
I could hear his eyes wander over the pages
and his thoughts bleeding through

while my sisters dove off the dock and
became fish with shimmering gills
like the trout with the hook in its throat
that I caught one morning
and tossed back into the lake as quickly as I could.

I come from a family of fishermen, whalers,
who swept up the Atlantic coast
claiming life and land.
It's in my blood.

But maybe it's not.
It's in my brother's blood
but not mine.

I preferred to sit on the lichen-laced ledges
and watch the fish dart to and fro
wagging their horny tails.
Nothing I could do would stop that.
Nothing I could do would stop my brother
or the blood that flowed through my veins
hissing family,
family,
family.

THE BED ON THE PORCH

I'd waited for what seemed like forever
to sleep on the bed on the porch.
Alone.

When my brother, the oldest,
got the first berth
I wanted like crazy to be him,
burrowed beneath the covers,
armed with a flashlight and a comic book,
a solitary soldier of the night.
It was a rite of passage.
My mother had done it, my uncle,
and my aunt before.

Now it was my turn.
I slipped beneath the sheets
and tugged on the blue felted blanket
from the mill where my grandmother worked,
stale smell of wool and camphor
trapped in the bedding.

I switched off the lights
and was plummeted into blackness.
But then my eyes grew accustomed to the dark.
Objects in the room sprang to life,
a blueberry rake framed on the wall,
the bow back chairs,
a half-finished jigsaw-puzzle
spread across the table.

When I dared to look out the large windows,
I felt the face of the world
peering in at me.
It was too close for comfort.

So I became a fox,
piquing my ears,
whetting my nails.
I grew a tail
and a snout.

And I caught the courage to sit up in bed
and stare out the window,
alert to the snap of a trout's tail hitting the water,
the croaking toads,
the call of the loons.

The lights from nearby cottages
cast thunderbolts across the water.
Night bugs hovered around the screens
pleading to enter.
Somewhere nearby, a night animal
burrowed into the hillside.
And the carpenter ants
came out of their torpor,
gnawing away.

But I kept watch through the long night.
And at dawn
I darted into my hole
and emerged from the covers,
triumphant.

WHERE THE BULLFROGS CROAK

Down where the bullfrogs ribbit,
amidst the rushes and the reeds that we folded into whistles,
live the pond lilies.
If you really want to see another world
that's the place to be,
beneath the large-leafed lily pads
and their fleshy, creeping underwater stems.
The mystery is that the lilies are closed all day.
At dusk they open,
each petal reclining blissfully,
bathed in moonlight.
It makes me want to stay up all night
to see what else conspires
in the murky, muddy deep.

ALL THAT WILDNESS

Maybe it was the heat,
or the lengthening days
stretched out like warm taffy,
but come July time slowed to a trickle.

I filled my pockets with patience and waited
for the wild blueberries to ripen
in the fields above the Olive Cottage.
It seemed like a lifetime—the grownups were always saying that,
but I didn't know what a lifetime was back then.
I didn't know it could be half a minute or half a century,
even twice that.

Then Dad came into the room
in his summer suit,
sky blue swim trunks and a white tee.
He said it was going to be a scorcher.
That was my cue.
I took my empty coffee can and headed up the dirt path
in my blue bellied Keds with white trim,
grinding the gravel underfoot.

I'd left my lethargy with the flagging fuchsia
and was alert as a cavefish
to all the wildness happening around me,
brambles shamelessly inching their way onto the path,
lichen trampling the stones,
the fizzy fragrance of pines.
A vortex of blackflies quivered before my eyes.
All around me was nature
determined to thrive.

I bounded into the field,
careful not to trample my prey.
And I chose a spot, lush and plentiful,
and sat back on my heels.
I started to fill my can
unaware that I was being watched.

Then a snake slithered round a rock,
eyeing me.
I got to my feet, unflinching,
as the snake wrapped its
tubular spine around my ankle.
Time stumbled and stopped.
But I would not shout.
I would not fear.
I would not give in.
I would stand my ground.

This was life,
fierce, intense.

I took a berry from my can
and popped it into my mouth,
relishing its sweet juice
and tangy flesh.
That was life too.

I kept right on eating those berries
until the snake unfurled itself and slithered off.
Then I crouched back down and filled my can to the brim.
I, too, could be determined.
I, too, could be wild.

THE WAY OF WORMS

My brother had a way with worms,
kneeling at the temple of dawn,
flecks of first light
scoring tree trunks.
He rocked back on his high-top sneakers with the golden stars,
the ones my mother said I couldn't have,
coaxing the worms from the soil,
snake charmer with only the song of his soul,
the breath of a blackbird,
and bowls upon bowls of gumption.

The spongy earth gave way,
and he plucked the worms from the soil
and dropped them into the ribbed coffee can.

My stomach turned.
Once I read that earthworms can remember for fourteen days.
But it wouldn't be that long.
They would finish hooked on a line,
in the mouth of a fish,
and all this long before the herring gull
could catch them in the act.

A CORN KIND OF DAY

Down the coast in Lincolnville,
next to the Olive Cottage,
there were corn kind of days and
lobster kind of days.

Corn days were lazy,
plain sailing, fern unfurling,
no bickering days.
They happened in late July
after an early evening shower
that stripped the air of static.
The locals parked their farm stands
in the thick of the green arrowed stalks
and sold their corn.

We pulled over in the Chrysler and
tumbled out of the car.
One by one we yanked back the
husks on the brown tasseled ears
checking for corn borers
and ripeness.

When we got the goods
we drove home,
corn and baked beans on our minds.
We kids would sit at the picnic table,
upright as the corn stalks.
And we'd start shucking,
blackflies barging in,
chewing holes in our ankles.
But we were oblivious.

The beans were in the oven,
the big pot of water rolling on the stove.
When it was time to eat
we sat at the long wooden table
on the porch,
cool as cukes.
And we ate in slow motion,
watching the sun drop behind the mile-high pines,
withering, vanishing day.

A Lobster Kind of Day

Lobster days were zesty,
fish jumping, pond simmering kind of days
with steam rising from the water's surface,
the flap trap of the screen door banging open and closed.
The kids were fighting over the hammock,
the dogs over a bone.

Mom was up early,
pot on the stove.
She had that expectant look on her face
like she was about to announce a big event.
She'd been craving lobster for days,
and that hankering hung in the air.
She sent dad into town, down to the pier
where pyramids of traps were stacked one atop the other.
He came back with the lobsters,
mottled shells,
squirming in brown, corded wrap.

I winced when she dropped them in the boiling water,
tails twitching,
striking the sides of the pot.
It was a minute, maybe,
before they were mute.

We ate outside at the picnic table,
coleslaw and lobster,
dipping the legs into butter,
sucking out the meat.
And in all the commotion it was easy to forget
that just a half hour ago the lobsters were as alive
as the day.

THAT KIND OF WOMAN

That woman I won't forget,
tangled somewhere up there
in the branches of the family tree.
She was a relative, not by blood,
but by proxy.

She golfed with my grandmother on weekends,
and on Wednesdays they would cart their
leaden balls with finger-sized craters
down to the bowling alley
where they had a hoot with the ninepins.
On Mondays they played bridge.

She liked a good yarn and devoured
romance novels
like chocolate
which she always
had on hand.

She was a real looker,
a free spirit,
men aplenty.
She was married but her husband was always away
on some mission outside of her orbit.

She was the kind of woman people talked about
when they had nothing better to do.
Rumor was that she'd had a child out of wedlock.
But she kept it hidden in her ample bosom
where there was usually a pack of Pall Mall's
and a lighter.

She liked to knit,
and she churned out Fishermen sweaters
with cables and bobbles
like she churned out stories of her travels,
to the Himalayas,
the Suez Canal.

She was that kind of woman
who knew how to live
and knew how to love,
and who could blame her for that.

WADERS AND FLAGS

It was a mystery,
whatever was in the big black dresser
in the back bedroom of the Olive Cottage.
We kids weren't supposed to open the drawers,
but one day I did.
I'd had enough of staring at their closed, straightlaced mouths.
After all I slept right next to the dresser,
in the black framed bed built by state prison inmates.
It was big enough for two with knobs on the headboard the size
of oranges.
Every night I watched the outline of the dresser blur and
vanish into the darkness
until there was nothing before my eyes.
but blackness.
How could it not make me think about what happened when
we died?

So one day I opened the drawers,
and I found a pair of waders
and the American flag that we raised each year
on the Fourth of July.
What was the big deal?
As if waders and flags were mysterious,
like my mother's cousin, Morris,
who went into the woods one day to hunt,
and was never seen again,
or whatever it was that Grandpa carried in his hip flask.
Why all these secrets
that pale so pitifully
next to the specter of death?

THE TOO MUCHNESS OF TOGETHERNESS

That particular day
I was transfixed on the two dragonflies,
piggybacked,
hovering above the picnic table,
laid out lovely
for Labor Day.
"Are they mating?" I wondered.

Friends, relations were arriving in droves
by water or land.
I could feel their gaze
boring through my flesh.
"Doesn't she have her mother's eyes?"

I looked away towards the water.
"I read that dragonflies lay their eggs in the pond."

"Why don't you go in?" said my aunt Doreen.
"Because I'm off with the dragonflies," I said silently.
"How long before their eggs will hatch?"

The wharf was getting crowded,
teetering,
woozy under the weight
of so many bodies.

Too many people,
too much noise.
"How long will the dragonflies stay here,
hanging in the air?"

"Party pooper," said my brother.
But I couldn't have cared less.
"How many legs does a dragonfly have?"
I squinted, zooming in on the furry spindles,
  gyrating in space.

Aren't you having fun?" asked a stranger.
"Do I look like I'm not having fun?" I said.
I was watching dragonflies and enjoying every minute.

The guests were complaining about too much food,
enough for an army.
But lunch hadn't even begun.
The dragonflies were separating now.
They were flying towards the pond,
and I was going with them.

One of them alighted on a wild rose branch,
bent over the water,
rainbow of hope.
"Is the female dropping her eggs?"
I thought.

I sat down on a nearby ledge
and watched the rose petals cleave
from their yellow seedy centers
and dive into the pond,
each like a tiny open palm wobbling on the waves.
If I could make myself small, I could be carried off with them.

Oh, I knew all about the birds and the bees,
and that all this commotion
started with two.
But I couldn't help but ask myself if, one day,
when I was one of two,
would I want all this togetherness?
Or would the dragonflies be enough.

HEAT WAVE

We woke up to the pond still as glass,
the temperature ramped up so high
you could fry an egg on your forehead.
My mother kept calling out, "One hundred and four degrees,"
merciless reminders that we were cooking.

We limped through the day,
zombie slugs,
sap sucked out of us
waiting for the snap.
It came around ten in the evening,
a wrinkle in the pond
and the air somersaulted.

I went out onto the wharf
to wait for the breeze to show its face.
It came in fits and starts.
But I welcomed it
like it was the Second Coming.

BY THE POND

I was always hanging out
at the rim of the pond
where the backwash percolated playfully
and the reeds grew fast and thick as nettles.
I'd whistle through a reed trapped between my thumbs
to catch the attention of the frog that ribbited unbrokenly,
no mind to this world
hanging on a thread.

Back at the cottage the grown-ups
would be lounging in the yard,
draped over chairs,
with their gin and tonics.
The kids would be banging around in the boathouse
building something,
a fort,
where I wasn't wanted.

But I was welcome
in the wetlands,
midst the stink of soggy turf
and a dozen forms of teeming life.
I wouldn't stir,
and if I did it was to bow down to the water sprites
or the silken entrails of cattails.
And I would understand
more than the ways of gin
or the wallop of hammer to nails.

THE FAIRY QUEEN

Even back then
I was a forest gal,
traipsing across fallen logs,
grinding my spine against rutted tree trunks
hoping to merge in some masterful way.

I'd get down on all fours and
comb through the mulch for artifacts,
sullying my nailbeds.
I was sure the tiny mounds of moss were fairy beds.

This was another world and I wished to be part of it.
If there were a crack in eternity, I was sure it was here,
in the forest, among the towering, majestic pines.
The deeper I went,
the more I believed
I could be master of my kingdom.

When I happened upon a pocket of silence,
distilled from a dozen sounds,
I built an altar,
and I decked it with feathers, stones, wildflowers,
a wand hewed from a branch, a leaf wet with dew.
And I summoned the wood sprites in my
small, sure voice.

That's when I heard a loud, labored hoot
that jarred my bones.
It was my brother.
He was laughing at me.
I stepped before him.

"The Fairy queen has come," I said,
and you should have seen his face.

SOMEONE

When I discovered the wooden hut,
hidden among the horsetail and hay,
I was steeped in a feeling of conquest,
flushed as a rose.

A rusty padlock dangled from the door,
sealed shut,
tight as a cork,
by time and debris.
The windows were smudged with grime and grease.
No welcome here.

I pressed my face into the glass.
I wasn't afraid of dirt.
Inside was a cot,
a Coleman stove,
a table with a pipe and three books,
and a solitary chair.
Some fishing gear leaned into a corner.

I liked to think that
the hut belonged to a
long lost relative I'd never met,
a kind-hearted soul
who loved the land like I did,
who didn't mind being alone with a pipe
and a book,
who didn't care for all the fuss and flurry
back at the Olive Cottage.

I could almost see him
through the bleary glass,
rising early,
time of still water,
brewing a coffee,
then heading out to pierce the dawn
with cool determination.

Someone who had decided
that this world
wasn't fit for him,
and who'd just picked up and
walked off.
just as summer did
when September came.

2

The Road to Rome

THE ROAD TO ROME

The car tires spin frantically,
bobbin-like,
along the road to Rome,
unravelling dreams and expectations.

The puckered pavement gnaws away at the rubber.
There's a crack or two,
just wide enough for a simple desire,
a life of goodness.

It's a one-way road,
no turning back,
It became that way the day I said, "I do."

I roll down the window to sip the air,
tepid, smoky, different than that
from where I came
an ocean away.
I thought I would be a turtle and bring my home with me.
In the end I brought empty space
waiting to be filled.

The car is a 1980 BMW.
Pier says it's the best model ever made.
I agree,
but not for its slick chassis
or its grinding guts,
but for the way it carries me surely and effortlessly
into the future.
The dashboard is laid out with precision,
oozing control.

I punch a button to turn on the radio.
Battisti is singing "Viaggiare."
In each note is the chink of the bangled bracelets
I was wearing the day we met.

Off to my left a Fiat 500 weaves recklessly
in and out of the tousled traffic.
No one keeps to single file in Rome.

A treacherous curve and I'm met
with a bouquet of flowers,
dried, pinched,
tacked to a tree trunk.

"Someone died there," says Pier.
And I say Hail Mary for a person I never knew,
except that it could be me
or you.
So many ways to die.

I turn my head for another glimpse.
But I can't stop the movement of my own life.

We swerve to miss a jackrabbit bounding across the road.
In my mind's eye I see its entrails plastered to the pavement,
my own in the face of an oncoming car.
But Pier turns the steering wheel
and we slide gracefully back into our own grove.
It's not my time.
Long live the rabbit.

Here's to a life of health and happiness.

OLEANDERS

I can never recall the name of the trees
that line the highway here,
ripping the eyes of drivers from the road
by doing nothing but being.

It's on the tip of my tongue,
but it slides into the fleshy part of my cheek
and is sent to some distal body part.

Pink blossomed they are,
clusters of gorgeousness
with long, tapered leaves,
butterknives poised for battle.
Imagine,
a single leaf, a shred of bark could kill.

The trees are guarding the sacred seam
where road becomes turf,
the rough junction
where man and nature meet,
where life and death collide.
I think if the road encroached any further
they would be ready with their poisoned pistols.

Oh yes,
it's the oleander.

THE AGONY OF NEWNESS

Here among the old
there is so much newness—
faces, words, tastes, smells, sights.
All this newness stings.
How long will it take for it to become ordinary?

Lumpy sidewalks with protruding elbows,
joints of tree trunks breaking through the pavement.
Will my feet ever get used to the uneven cobblestones,
the way they drink coffee here
in short, quick gulps?

And the lateness.
No one is ever on time.
It's no place for the March Hare.

Reaching out my foot and touching his body each night,
I, who was accustomed to and cherished my own space,
my bed, my private world of dreams.
It's a dilemma, how singular becomes plural with ease.

Cathedrals, ruins, marble statues.
All this old that is unfamiliar to me.

Sitting down at my makeshift desk,
a wooden door, poised on sawhorses,
cracked paint crying for attention.

The rude coolness of the marble surfaces,
the rickety old stove hiked up on one side,
and the fickle flame of the gas burner.

The distance from all the things I once knew and loved.
The absence of family, friends, familiar haunts and habits.

How long will it take to get used to being pulled
in every direction,
the ache of my senses stretched by newness?

Growing pains,
metamorphosis
this act of becoming.

How long will it take for theirs to become mine?

How Different We Are

Time and time again I ask myself
why is it that my desires are less important than his.
He doesn't state them in big words and loud ways
but in sure, determined movements.

And when he asks me what I want,
and I dare to tell him the truth,
he turns it on its head,
magician like,
and feeds me the wants of his own will,
making them look like they're mine.
For a moment I pause to consider
if he knows better than I.
And in that tiny breach of time
my desires fly out the window.

How different we are.
I like the rattle of the cutlery from the coffee bar below,
the chirp of the birds at dawn.

He hates the riffle of turning pages,
the click of my knitting needles,
the chatter of diners at a nearby table.

I long for light.
He craves darkness.

I dream of a life rooted to the soil,
where I can see myself in
every spear of uncut grass.

He dreams of a life in limbo,
traveling the globe,
searching for a place that settles his soul.
I guess everyone is looking for somewhere to call home.

PLINKTOLOGY

I fold shut the wooden doors of the cranky elevator.
Its diamond shaped metal ribs contract,
pinching my thoughts.
Otis.
It's written on a tiny brass plaque under the floor buttons.
The world is smaller than I thought.
The elevator belches and starts upward,
then stops abruptly.
PLINK!

I step out
reminding myself I'm on precarious ground,
married now,
my soul tethered to another,
another place,
another way of life.

I slink, cat-like, from one room to the next of my new home,
marking my territory.
The living room is a marvel,
pentagon shaped,
with floor to ceiling windows and a narrow balcony
scattered with pine nuts.
One falls, hitting the wrought-iron railing.
PLINK!
a happy omen I trust.

I push open the bathroom door and stand before the sink.
A bobby pin,
mind of its own,
frees itself from my rumpled hair

and dives downward into the metal drainpipe.
PLINK! PLINK!
a morse code
waking the downstairs neighbor.

I kneel to lift the ugly sap-colored carpet
and tap my nail against a loose floor tile.
I jiggle it loose and peer into the
the space below,
utter darkness,
perhaps a portal to other realms.
Don't wake me from my dream.

In the bedroom I throw open the window shutters,
my eyes tripping over the scabs of gray paint on the slats.
The sky assaults me, achingly white.
Stillness,
an easy rustling,
then PLINK!
my first drop of Roman rain.

I THOUGHT I KNEW OLD

The Roman sky is really something,
pink at dawn, threaded with orange ribbons,
indigo at dusk,
raging with starlings.

And the ruins,
I've never seen anything like them,
temples of blanched stone
that sprout from the landscape
amidst the scarlet poppies
bold and clever enough to grow everywhere.
I wish I were like that.
I'm clever but I'm not brave enough to grow anywhere,
anyhow,
or anyway.
I'm not numb to the pain of change.

I thought old was my childhood neighbor
with her baked sourdough breath.
She sat on the sofa, legs folded beneath her,
knitting socks,
day in, day out.
I still have a pair of them.
But she wasn't old,
not like these ruins,
rooted in eternity.

I'm ironing one of Pier's shirts,
my eyes trailing a clutch of clouds tugged across the sky by
a heavenly breath.
Back in New York I dropped my shirts at the launderers,

picked them up
creased and pleated.
I used to stand on a stool and iron my father's handkerchiefs.
But I'd never ironed a man's shirt.
I never imagined it would make me cry.
But it does

And it makes me want to capture
the steamy vapors of my own breath in a bottle
and leave it in a crypt to grow old,
and I mean really old,
like these ruins.

LAUNDRY

In Rome I fell in love with a street
not because of where it took me,
or for the light that dazzled the rooftops,
or the salmon color of the buildings
that made me think of warm flesh.
I loved it for the lines of laundry strung across the balconies
to dry,
sheets, towels, pajamas,
sleeveless men's undershirts.

Sometimes they hung still,
casting a mood of contemplation.
But when the wind rose
the sheets puffed up with laughter,
the towels and pajamas thrashed mirthfully.
"Let's live it up!" they said.

I didn't know to whom they belonged.
But I felt like I did.
And at dusk when they settled,
in my tiny human mind,
they became prayer flags,
spreading the words of grace and good will.

HOLY

Here
in this place
everything is holy.
The temples, shrines, statues,
the churches on every corner,
the ancient trees,
gentle giants that squat to stay upright,
even the mounds of dog shit on the sidewalks.
the pitted streets,
the crippled stairwells,
remembrance in every step,
the honking cars,
the brittle buses that creak at every turn, jarring my bones,
the stinking rubbish that spills from cannisters
into the streets,
the coffee with its halo of steam,
a passing stranger who smiles and says, "Buongiorno,"
the scrappy cats that roam the ruins,
the starlings that circle at dusk,
all holy.
Even me, who grew up as far from God as the devil's pitchfork,
raised on books, brains, and brawn.
That was my Trinity,

I like this holiness,
this hallowed haze that seeps
from sidewalks and sewers alike.
Yes,
everything here is holy,
and maybe that's how it should be.

I Saw It in the Movies

I saw it in the movies,
the Italian mother at the stove, her torso tucked into a pinafore,
waving a wooden spoon,
orchestrating something bigger than life
called a meal.

The family sat around the table,
their lilting language like a lullaby,
one word fitting into the other as pleasingly as puzzle pieces.

But then their voices rose
and their bodies bent,
gesticulating wildly.
Who says you can't love while arguing?

The woman who ruled the roost
set a bowl of pasta on the table.
The room grew still,
and the bowl was passed,
a sacred vessel of adoration.
Buon appetito!
Let the feast begin.
I'd never seen people eat with such gusto
or reverence.

THE THING ABOUT WISHES

No need to ask if I tossed a coin into the Trevi Fountain.
I tossed two.
Doesn't everyone?
Of course, everything had to be just right,
like that time on Midsummer's Eve
when we gathered on a hill
and lit a bonfire.
All high we were on hope and hankerings.
We wrote down our desires on parchment lanterns
and we wished beyond wild
for things that didn't even exist.
We sent the lanterns adrift and watched them float
far off,
on beyond zebra.
And we told ourselves if our wishes didn't happen now
they would happen later.

When I tossed my coins into the Trevi Fountain,
I'd waited for a clear night,
peppered with stars and a slice of moon,
the ruckus of the city ebbing.
And I planted myself in the pavement,
my back to the roaring rivers.
And I wished for a life of love.

I closed my eyes and imagined what it would be like
to embrace both gain and pain,
victory and defeat,
the beautiful and the ugly,
all things great and small,
and feel blessed at the same time.

I determined to love
no matter what.
And when I'd stepped into this vision
and made it mine,
I tossed my two coins over my shoulder,
into the roaring water.

CATACOMBS

Down the road from where I live
are the catacombs of Priscilla.
I went there one day
thinking I'd explore the ancient tombs.
A guide led me into the subterranean canals.
At first I walked charily, head bent,
measuring my footsteps
for fear of tripping into the past.

I scanned the pastel wall paintings,
the relics,
the bones.
And I thought
where am I?
What world is this?

Then I got plucky and reached out to touch the walls.
I adjusted my vision
in hopes of glimpsing a spirit
who could tell me that life was eternal
and immortality was not just a dream.
But as my fingertips met the powdery stone
my guide said, "Don't."

Via Adda

At the end of my street
that's not really mine
except that I've walked it so often that it feels like part of me.

At the end of my street
I come to a rectangle, roped off with sticky tape.
Inside there's the outline of a man sketched with white chalk.
A passerby tells me someone was killed there last night.
I can't believe I was so near and heard nothing, felt nothing
because sleep had me.

I peel my eyes from the umbra of the chalk figure,
an ugly truth of earthly life,
and divert them to the red poppies sprung up next to a nearby
ruin.
All I see are their bobbing heads.
Sleep
Peace
Death
Remembrance.
I will not take my eyes from the poppies until they become
mine.

ABOUT CLAY

Twice a week I take the bus to the center of the city,
to the hole in the wall where I do pottery.
I shake, rattle, and roll to the bus's
jerky movements.
It's funny seeing the people climb aboard
and anchor themselves to walls, chairs,
anything they can get their knuckles into.
It takes a hell of a lot of time to get there
because the traffic's as thick as locusts
and the bus as slow as sculpting sadness.
But when I arrive, I'm good.

"Hey," I say to Victoria.
She owns the hole in the wall.
It's where she casts women from cylinders
that she pulls up on the wheel.
I'm never sure if I like them or not.

I take a slab of clay and start to wedge it on a wooden table
trying to be forceful but gentle at the same time,
not like my mother when she kneaded bread.
She was like a tornado coming off the prairie,
and I was afraid to watch her,
pulling and punching.
I felt bad for the dough
when I probably should have felt bad for her.

I slap the clay onto the wheel
and start it spinning.
Its gritty grains burn the creases of my palms.

I make mostly vessels,
bowls, pitchers, mugs.
I tell myself it's because we don't have that many
and we're living on a shoestring.
But I think it's because I have ideas for my new life
and I want to store them in containers,
as many as I can
lining the shelves.

But if I never made a thing
I think it would be enough,
digging my hands into the clay,
culling the seeds of groundedness, growth, new life.
Maybe one day I will like Victoria's women.
And one day I will forgive my mother for how she treated the
dough.

CHILD OF FIRE

You would have thought something was ending,
the smell of burning mug wort,
the baleful way the smoke curled into clenched fists.
the cries of pain that ripped through the room.

I sat on the edge of the bed,
big bold belly about to burst.
He knelt at my foot holding a burning stub of moxa to my toe.
Knowing him, he was praying at the same time.
Meanwhile, the doctor needled the tips of my shoulders.
It could have been a tribal ritual, a trial of torture,
but it was a birth.

A few months back this baby was just a thought.
Now it struggled to come forth like one of those ideas
for a picture book that got tangled in the weedy wickets
of my mind.

I knew what I was in for.
He was going to be a Sagittarian,
and a beauty
because we'd needled the beautiful baby point for months.
When he came down the birth canal,
head round as a pumpkin,
man, it burned.
Child of fire, I thought,
and I was right.
You knew it when he let loose his first cry,
hot tempered, impatient.
But I walked straight into the flames
like any mother would.

THE THINGS WE TELL OURSELVES

I told myself that if I could find a bird's nest with just one egg
then my world would be set aright.
You know what it's like.

We'd been fighting about something that didn't matter,
not like birds' eggs anyway
or the geraniums on the balcony
with their spellbinding bustles of blooms
that I pruned each Sunday.
I'd journeyed deep into the heart of this person
and I'd come to a place that said,
"Danger."
"Electricity."
"Do not enter."
But I paid no heed.
The sparks flew
and we both got burned.

It was easy enough to bandage my wounds.
But I was not skilled enough to close the gap
that leaked his hurts
that came long before me.
I told myself I needed a witch doctor,
or maybe a bird's nest.
And I went to the park.
I found a nest in the bend of an elderberry.
It looked like a filigree jewel!
Inside was a small green egg.

I kept watch for three long days.
But on the fourth day the cat got there before I did.
And you know what happened.
What had I expected?
It's all about survival.

The cat was just surviving.
He was just surviving.
That was the last time I got burned.

How We Made Books

He came in the early mornings,
just after the behemoth of a garbage truck passed,
gobbling up the bins, emptying them into its greedy gut
and spitting them back onto the street.
He parked his van across the way,
in the driveway of the grand villa
with the roaring lions at the gate.
The owners let him do that because they loved art.

The van was a white Mercedes.
He was German after all.
He'd converted it into a studio,
with magnetic walls to affix his paintings.
And he'd peopled it with brushes, palettes, and paper.
He sketched all morning.
I wrote.

At noon he brought me his work.
We spread it across the crystal table that sat
on cheap cement pedestals that I'd bought for a dime
and stained a mottled yellow.
And we talked about pages, light, color,
words, meanings.
Sometimes a person or an object from his life or mine
found its way onto the canvas.

Then we had some lunch
and talked some more
about his cats, and his gal
and my guy and my child on the way
and the other already here

and what I thought of Bonnard
and if he missed home.

After lunch he went back to his van
to paint some more.
He stayed put until the starlings gurgled and took to the sky.
Then we met again
before each image and word.
We cut and we pasted
until it all looked good.
And that's how we made books.

BARGAINING

You can't pick and choose,
you couldn't back then anyway.
I wanted another boy,
another Sagittarian.

I locked eyes with the stars,
bargained with the cosmos
proffering my unfleeting attention.
And then, it happened.
I was pregnant again.

It started off all right
but then I spent four months in bed
watching my belly swell and bulge,
mapping the movements of a hand or foot
prodding my flesh.

I talked to my baby about the weather,
the bird that tottered on the telephone wire
outside the window,
the brook that gabbled and burped at the close of each day,
his brother, his father, our friends.

I told the baby what this world was like
and I think the little rascal heard me
because at seven months
I felt the tightening,
then a jab in my lower back.
This baby wanted out.

At the hospital they prepped to shoot me up with cortisone,
puff up the baby's lungs.
But I didn't want that.
So I bargained with the doctor,
and I struck up a deal with fate.

I bargained with my babe,
pleading with him to hang on,
just another month.
I did what I said I wouldn't,
promising him the moon and the stars,
knowing I had no power over their gyrations.

I guess he was a good listener,
because he stilled for twenty-four hours.
I returned home and went to bed.
I stopped whining and wishing
and I read to my baby.
He stayed put for fifty-five more days,
no need for needles,
no need for smoke,
He started to descend on the cusp,
then slowed his journey
and entered the world as a Sagittarian.
I'd won the bargain.
And he'd taught me to listen.

FRIENDS OF THE HEART

Those days when the earth cracked open
and sent up a heat wave
I thought it couldn't get any hotter.
But it did.
The guy on the radio said, "Stay inside,"
but we didn't listen.
We climbed into the BMW
and swung into the traffic on the ring road,
thinking we could outrun the heat.

No way, no how.
It was anchored to the day
with the tenacity of Saint Clare.

We were going to Campo di Mare.
We knew when we got closer to the sea,
because there was the eggy smell of sand,
the sting of citrus,
the caravan of bicycles pedaling through the heat wall.
We parked in front of the house,
rubbing up against the jasmine that leeched from the fence.

The kids ran into the yard
and in three shakes were as pink and sandy as turnips
just pulled from the soil.
They didn't care about the heat.
But we, the adults, sat on the porch and talked about it
like it would go away if we complained enough.
Had it ever been like this?
Of course, it had.
But we'd forgotten,

like we forget about heartbreak,
the pains of labor.
Otherwise, how would we keep on living?

In the garden, the lemons sweat on the branches,
drizzling their juice onto the stinging nettles.
The plums and peaches stewed on the vines,
and the charred basil hurt my eyes.

We made lunch and ate at the round table with the plastic cloth,
covered with bluebells that made me think of home.
Then sometime mid-afternoon the stillness snapped.
And we put on our swimsuits, rolled our towels,
and headed for the beach.
It was the first time I'd seen black sand.
All I could think of was Pompeii, scalding heat,
and melting bodies.

We couldn't wait to wade into the lukewarm ocean
and dive into the deep, searching for coolness
like it was buried treasure.
Then we emerged, huddled under an umbrella
and watched the kids chase the tide
and dig for creatures in the sand.

Back home we played badminton on the lawn,
and decided to let the heat be.
We gathered around the table with a deck of cards
and drank iced coffee.
And the kids fell asleep draped over the lawn chairs.
Friends of the heart we were.
And I would think to myself
who could wish for more.

MOVING ON

When I packed up the rooms
I left a pool of water in the marble sink,
a bird feeder on the windowsill,
a few breaths in the bellows.
I did it purposefully.

I took a crystal doorknob that spun loosely
from its threads,
an extra tile from the marble floor,
a pot that wasn't mine
where I'd grown basil and thyme.

I hated sucking the life out of my space,
packing it in cardboard boxes and plastic wrap.
I hated walking through the vacant rooms,
thwacked by the echo of emptiness,
the outlines of furniture visible on the
faded floor.
I hated my attachment to the walls.

After nine years
we were moving on,
leaving la bella vita
for la vie en rose.
We were going to the south of France.
I was doing it again,
leaving home, haunts, friends,
departing the holy city.

There were the awkward,
heart-wrenching farewells

as we cleaved ourselves from
that life,
and the ill-fitting unease
as we thought about thrusting
ourselves into another.

I didn't have the nerve to close the door
behind me.
So I left it wide open.
But as soon as I'd stepped into the elevator
a breeze wafted in and shut it for me.

3

LA MAISON DES REVES

(THE HOUSE OF DREAMS)

MY HOUSE

My house sits in the lap of the dragon,
built upon shelves of sandstone
that surfaced after the dragon swallowed the sea,
or so they say.
Because once upon a time the Mediterranean covered the land,
long before the gulls dropped eggs in briar baskets,
before the trees got any idea of creeping down hillsides,
long before the thought of me even took shape.

I heard from a neighbor,
who heard from her mother,
who heard from an uncle,
that the roof of my house was laid on a clear day,
when the sun pierced a hole in a lemony sky,
when you could see the belly of Corsica
puffed up on the horizon.

In the hills behind my house there's a basin that yawns wide.
It's a bunker from the Second World War,
a sanctuary for soldiers to refurbish their supplies
and their faith.
Their remains are locked in the stone,
in some mystical matrix of memory,
or so they say.

I walk miles from one room of my home to the next,
treading the path of children, guests.
And I wonder,
what does it take to really get to know this space,
to really get to know anything or anyone,
to peer into an object or a person's face

and adjust your vision so finely
that you see yourself looking back?

I could get lost in the galaxy of elliptical spheres and comets
sketched in the wooden floorboards,
the piles of rubble everywhere,
elaborately labelled,
when one word would suffice.
Past.

This morning I watched a spider crawl
from the neck of a desk lamp to the corner of the room.
The time it took seemed no more than that from birth until now,
a contraction that rudely abbreviated my existence.

I take a book from a shelf and open it across my knees.
A silverfish walks through the pages and settles between a split
verb,
unaware.
Unaware is what the world is,
or so they say.
Unaware of the possibility in each second, each shape, each
sound, color, or breath.

On a windy day, the shutters on my windows break free
and fly open.
They're a peculiar color blue,
peculiar, because I don't know what it is,
but I know what it's not.

We don't really know what life is, do we?
The world is asleep,
or so they say,

having forgotten that all it takes is a true and gentle touch,
a kiss on the hem of desire
for the world to awaken.

A hundred years from now when my house is no more,
when my soul has flown into the ether.
what will they say?

STONE SOUP

Imagine,
streets lined with orange trees,
white buds bursting into a star shower,
flurrying like snow.
The first time I saw them I thought I was tripping.

It took me back to the time I rolled a joint in the woods,
at the crack of dawn, in a pickup truck.
My own words crinkled in my ears,
and the pine forest became a citrus grove,
dripping with fruit.
I promised myself never to smoke pot
or eat an orange again.

But wouldn't you know it.
I bought a house in the south of France
with an orange tree right off the kitchen.
The tree was magnificent,
a grand master,
one hundred years old.

I found myself clinging to its roots,
beguiled by its beauty,
aching to belong.

When I moved in, I blessed my new home,
misting holy basil,
tossing salt in each corner,
chimes and buddha bowls in every room.
And I scribbled a benediction on parchment paper,
and buried it beneath the orange tree.

I threw myself into gardening,
digging deep into the earth,
soiling my half-moons,
each time depositing a grain of me next to a seed or sapling,
taking a stone in return and placing it on a shelf.

Many moons later,
when dusk was busy sweeping away the crumbs of day,
I headed to the garden to reap my rewards,
white-bodiced, peach-faced turnips,
carrots alongside their ghostly neighbors—parsnips,
beet greens and chives.
I chopped them and tossed them into a boiling pot of broth.
Then I took a stone from the shelf
and dropped it into the stock,
hoping that it would nourish my bones,
and I, too, would take root in this foreign soil.

PALM TREES

I live in the land of palm trees,
bushy bonnets perched on dimpled stalks of peach fuzz.
On a calm day the fronds reach out and touch one another,
linking hands along the shore,
smiling for the camera.

But I've seen palm trees after a rough night,
bearded and disheveled,
shedding like those cats that wander across the threadbare
winter lawn.
I've seen them after their season of glory.

I had a palm tree on my front lawn, long and lithe,
with a glorious head-dress
and dates that dangled teasingly from its loins.
It bent and swayed freely,
a true libertine.
Sometimes it leaned so far to the left I was sure it would snap,
taking down the house with it.

By day it bounced boisterously,
netting butterflies and breezes.
At night it peered through the windows shamelessly,
watching us sleep.
I found its antics charming,
and I named it George after the third son I couldn't have.

A bird lived somewhere among its dried thatch.
And one day it tsked the entire day,
drilling a hole in my brain.
I asked myself what that was all about.

That night there was a storm.
It blew in with a mighty mojo,
hitching a ride on the waves,
flinging pebbles,
paving the streets in stones.
It tore through town, foaming at the mouth,
snatching palm fronds, hurling them every which way.
And I worried what nature had in mind.
"Don't take it personally," hissed the wind.
But I did.

The next day I surveyed the battlefield of slayed foliage,
slim stalks angled every which way,
headless trunks,
wanton destruction.
It was ugly.

And there was George, arched over drunkenly,
head on the roof.

We had no choice but to chop the tree down.
But I planted bulbs around the stump.
"In loving memory of a dear friend."
In the spring when the bulbs bloomed
I knew what it was all about.
Creation.

THE REBELLION

I should have known
the morning the workers arrived,
tap dancing in on their steel-toed boots,
tipping their hard hats to the day.
"Bonjour."
We had decided to build a veranda,
mindless of the opposition.

The protests began with the wood lice,
miniature cannons
rolled up on the walkway.

A fleet of armored beetles
descended on the stone tarmac,
shimmering unnervingly.

Lizards bolted from their bunkers
and stationed themselves on the parapets,
bellies to the ground,
snipers, taking aim,
their commander in chief a black cat, hunch-backed on the wall,
eyes crunched in disapproval.

I thought about running for cover.
Only the snails initiated a slow retreat,
inching towards the neighbor's lawn in pairs.

When the work started
my feathered friends fled,
assaulted by the death rattle of the cement mixer,
the hyphenated brrr of the pneumatic drill.

Then a dozen volcanoes erupted on the lawn,
as the ants began a mass exodus,
striking out in single file.

I suppose I hadn't given it enough thought.
I was encroaching on another's territory,
disrupting, displacing, a way of life,
its rhythms and rituals,
comings and goings,
right there in my yard.
Shame on me.

When the work was finished, I called a truce.
But the wood lice and beetles stood their ground.
The ants engineered a steady patrol across the doorway,
the lizards lay low in the gutters,
and I wished for a dove or an olive branch.

In the end,
they forgave me,
parting peaceably,
with visiting rights only.

I no longer wish for an olive branch,
but for their gracious way of acceptance.

WISTERIA

I watch the wisteria thread its way through the curves of the
iron fence,
basting its handsome tresses onto the spires.
It climbs to the top of the cypress,
gathering the bald-headed cones into its fold,
preaching beauty and promise from a makeshift pulpit.
And it occurs to me that maybe it's the wisteria
that holds life together.

One day it entered without knocking,
and slung its perfumed pendulums over the arm
of a porch chair.
I stopped what I was doing
and followed its beckoning tendrils.
It lured me into paradise.
More than once I stumbled over its loveliness as it led me
into a holy space,
a grove of thick bamboo shoots,
windpipes, sprouting from the turf,
earthen vases and tiny temples of twigs
that could only have been built by wood sprites or fairies.
The birds were aflutter,
urging my spirit to run free.
But I sat down at an old marble table with two rusty chairs.
It wasn't long before the wisteria joined me.

FOOTSTONES

Once it happened that I wandered high above the hillside,
hoping to catch a glimpse of heaven.
I traipsed through the ferns,
their feathery fronds clamoring for my attention.
I snagged my muslin shirt on the prickly paw
of a paddle cactus
and caught a wide-eyed sunflower glaring at me.
When I ducked into the weedy wickets of bramble,
I felt the ill-mannered nudge
of a pebble in my shoe.
I looked down to discover a step.
Beneath me, the sills of sandstone sloped into a secret staircase
that descended to the sea.

I forgot all about heaven and followed it.
Down, down, down,
swept up in that vertiginous movement of snowflakes and rain,
the spin of gravity that calls to be loved and hated
at the same time,
if that's at all possible.

It led me all the way to the shore
where the tide had been hoarding pebbles and stones
all through the night.

I sifted through them, searching for thin slices of granite.
And one by one I flicked them into the sea.
They became flying saucers, in an alien land,
skimming the plucky surface of the waves.
And I thought to myself,
What is life if you haven't skipped stones?

I kicked off my shoes and waded into the waves.
When I came out, I was wearing sand slippers.
Then I lay down and spread my arms and legs wide.
And I made an angel in the sand.
I'd caught my glimpse of my heaven.

ONCE

Once in a blue moon
the equator tightens its belt,
the seasons burst their boundaries,
and it snows here
in the land of lemons.

The flakes start sparingly,
eddying earthward,
then thicken,
clumping on doorsteps,
curdling on the curbs,
taking hostage all rhyme and reason.

The white mantle on the stone walls is hopelessly lovely,
the citrus trees, turned ashen,
trembling for their lives,
not so.

One thought permeates the air.
What is the world coming to?

The last time it happened the pond froze over, stilling time.
I tottered on the rim of its rimy surface,
startled by a stirring beneath its frozen lid.
And I knelt, poking my fist through a wafer of ice
into the churning water coming up for air.
A fish broke the surface,
and I reached out and caught a corner of its thready gills.
"Take me with you," I said.
But it dove back under,
leaving a hush in its wake.

Soon the silence was severed by the sweet-tie song
of my treasured neighbor,
the chickadee.
And I shifted my gaze upward to its black capped head
tilted towards the brittle, wintry sky.
The snowflakes were melting,
closing the portals of possibility.
The citrus trees would be saved,
and I would keep my human form.

MILLY MOON-FACE

One night a moonchild came to me,
bleary eyed and pink cheeked.
Her name was Milly Moon-face.
It was right after the Spring Equinox.

I'd said goodnight to the cream-skirted daffodils
beneath the window,
the quacking froglets in the creek,
the March hare who leapt across the pages of a book
tossed in the folds of the bedcovers.

I'd said my prayers and was entering the land of dreams
when Milly Moon-face whispered to me
in a cool, come-hither voice,
prying me from my slumber.
I freed myself from the tangle of the sheets
conspiring to keep me in.

When she let down a ladder, crafted from moonbeams,
I grasped the golden rungs and climbed upwards.
Soon I was catapulting into space,
caught up in cosmic currents.
"Where are we going?" I asked Milly Moon-face.
"Nowhere," she cooed.

I knew when we'd gotten to nowhere
because my clothes dropped away into nothingness,
then my skin,
my bones,
and even my organs.
I watched them float into oblivion

with eyes that were no longer mine.
All that was left was my heart, pulsating,
next to the stars.

I shrunk to the size of a pinpoint.
But then as I became less, I became more,
my bodyless being swelling into an endless mass
in a dazzling display of divine logic,
growing until a burst of light broke through the blackness,
wakening me.

I sat up in my own bed and got hold of my racing heart.
I checked to see if I was clothed.
I adjusted my head on my shoulders.
I seemed to be in one piece
But something had changed.

I will never forget Milly Moon-face.

Daybreak

I slip out long before the world is awake
and hastily mount the stone steps.
I want to be the first one there.
But I meet a grasshopper on the way,
clipped to a spindle of grass.
"Come along," I say.

Then my eyes trip over a lizard,
trailing me,
wide-eyed and watchful.

A rapscallion kitten,
just tumbled from a litter,
tags along,
swatting a butterfly with its fledgling paw.

We edge along the rock wall,
a merry caravan of pilgrims,
eager to witness the birth of day

When we reach the summit, a seagull greets us
from its roost on a stump.
I lower my head and
clasp the hand of the eucalyptus.
And we stand there on the precipice of dawn,
beholding the flushed sky as it turns to amber.

When the sun lifts its bowed chin and floats upward,
it breaks my heart.

STILL

I wake to find the world dangerously still,
flattened against a cottony sky.
Lavender spears slouched against the stone wall,
Japanese lanterns plumped up, holding their breath,
a gecko neatly pressed into a crease of the windowsill,
all unmoved by my stares.
I swear the world has come to a halt.

The wind chimes hang numbly from the crooked arm
of an olive tree,
a sure sign of gravity,
and the gravity of the moment.

I turn my ear to catch the scolding chant of the brown thrasher,
tsk, tsk, tsk,
the brisk shrug of the gull's wings before it takes flight.
But my senses alight on the dull throb of emptiness,
and I place my hand on a chapped bow of the orange tree,
searching for a pulse.

I dare not take the rake and score the earth
or attempt to trim the frayed hem of the thyme.

So I go about my day,
grinding coffee beans,
pressing them into the sieve of the moka.
I split two rumpled cardamon pods,
empty them into my cup of brew,
and I go to the window.
I sip my coffee and as it slips down the back of my throat
the stillness is ripped open by a black dart.

A crow touches down,
planting its nubby claws into a drugget of tousled grass.

I spot a fiddlehead pushing through the soil
and the world rejoices.
The fronds of the palm tree billow upwards.
The shiver of the wind chimes becomes a tinkle.
The lavender straightens its spine.
And I put down my coffee cup
and accept the invitation to pick up my rake.

APRIL

It's always momentous, when the crocuses break through the
stiff earth
and the moory scent of buried time percolates to its surface,
a muddy marshland,
quicksand beneath my feet.
For a few seconds I wish to be sucked under
into the earth's chambers,
down to the source of the infinite,
where life lives,
and death dies.

I squint to see the invisible hand
that peels away the layers of winter
to reveal the fresh flesh of spring,
bright-faced buds wrapped in tight jackets, slick as youth,
bleeding their colors from winter's wounds.

The tightly coiled fiddleheads loosen their grip,
releasing a bitter smelling salt
that coats the pussy willows
which, if you ask me,
should be called rabbits feet.

I am tempted to suture the cracks,
lest the colors leak into my memory,
wakening the long-lost lilies.

Don't get me wrong.
I love the Spring.
It's just that my father passed away in April,
shot by a gunman.

He drowned in a puddle of blood,
his ear to the pavement.
In a mere moment he leapt through autumn and summer,
into winter,
the season of slumber.

When the crocuses begin to unwind
I climb the hillside to witness the coming
of the archangel flowers
with their buttery wings and bowed heads,
the crumpled faces of the crimson poppies, startled from sleep.
What more do I need to believe in resurrection?

THE NOBLE FIG TREE

There is no denying the fig tree.
When I lean into the curve of its arched spine
and it turns a large eared leaf towards me
I wonder if you can love a tree as much or more than a person.

I insist on being present when the fig tree gives birth
to its first fruits,
silk-skinned teardrops
that blossom again and again
into a rich violet hue.
I catch my breath when they tumble to the ground
in the noble art of letting go.

I didn't taste a fig until I was a grown woman,
coming as I did from the land of snow crusted orchards,
crisp apples, and mealy pears.
I will never forget my first bite,
moist and seedy,
a forbidden fruit if there ever was one.
It spoke to me of faraway places, lips parted, talking in tongues.

As Fall draws to a close,
battening down its hatches,
I gather the last of the figs in the bosom of my apron.
I station myself at the stove
and I stir their pulp into a sugary paste.
From the corner of my eye, I watch the last of the fig leaves
writhe and twitch
in a motion I know is a prelude to yet another death,
a little death,
if there is such a thing.

I can the compote and set it on the pantry shelf.
And I remind myself that it won't be long before the wood
sorrel sprouts on the hill,
and the fig tree's sparse winter skeleton shudders,
stretching its spindly fingers upward,
rising on its haunches to new life.

I must remember to tell my children
to make my final bed under the noble fig tree
where I know its gentle breath will
ease me into my own little death.

WE LIED

We said we would never lie to our kids.
We made that vow when we were
unseasoned singles,
alien to parenthood.

But then we got a dog from the shelter,
a brown-eyed bastard
with a tail that ticked like
a metronome.

His name was Millou.
We loved to play ball with him,
to pet him,
and to sing him to sleep.

But Millou had a different way of loving.
He barked too loudly,
a boisterous baritone,
when anyone passed.
He dug too deeply when he buried a bone.
And he chewed too eagerly
on the kids' checkered shirts,
shredding the cloth into coat tails.

We tried to show him another way
but he wouldn't listen.
One day he ran off,
and was found in the aisle of a department store,
chomping on a shoe.

We drove into town and picked him up.
Seeped in sorrow,
we took him to back to the shelter
where they told us he'd been beaten in his former home.

When the boys asked where Millou was,
we lied.
We said he'd gone back to his mother.
We didn't have the heart to let on yet
that in this precious world
there was a different way of loving.

MURMURATION

Each evening at dusk
the swallows gather in numbers,
heedless of the curfew.
And they murmurate.

It's a curious occurrence,
the sky, a giant etcher sketcher,
birds swaying to and fro across its screen,
seeking safety in numbers
when we find safety in few.

Each time they turn my heart flutters,
beholding that moment of communion.

Who hasn't wanted to fly at least once?
I wish for it each night,
my brain afire as I frame my desire in a golden orb
and anchor it deep in my heart.

And then it happens,
in a dream within a dream.
I lift my arms and like wings they propel me skyward.
I fly into a boundless breadth,
attached to nothing
but part of all.

When I awaken,
all I want is to join the swallows,
to murmurate,
in a world where one becomes many
and many become one,
where there is safety in numbers.

IF WISHES WERE HORSES

Today he took half an interest
in what I was doing,
asking me what I was writing.

But he doesn't care about the process,
the mind-bending cycle of death and renewal
that belongs to creation.
He is only concerned with the outcome.

I can't say I blame him.
He doesn't have the hardware
or the patience to delve deep,
to observe the unfolding of a thought,
to examine it through a prism,
parachuting to the place of just-rightness.

I wish he could feel the agony of my missteps,
my unabashed joy when the freesia blooms.
I wish he could celebrate things
that haven't yet happened,
like I do,
release his gallant grip long enough to become
a dandelion puff, bedazzled by a breeze.
But it's like my father used to say.
If wishes were horses
beggars would ride.

So I leave it alone.

Spring Cleaning

I skim the winter scraps,
the parched casements and ribbed skeletons of tree pods,
from the supple surface of the puddle pond.
And I prune the fruit trees, all skin and bones,
and edge the ragged garden beds.

I hose down the shed, reluctantly wiping the cat's paw prints
from the panes of freckled glass.
Then I head to the house,
flinging open the windows,
airing the bedding,
taking special care with the pillows
where the heads of my dear ones have lain,
doing my best to extract the essence of love
from the feathers and fuzzballs.
Yesterday seems ages ago.

I empty the drawers, anointing them with lavender and rose
wood oil,
rearranging their contents,
instating a new world order.
The mateless socks say it all.
I pause to picture them wandering the earth looking for the
perfect partner.
The perfect partner—what an idea!

I floss the chair slats,
coax the dust bunnies from the corners
and pen them in my dustpan.
Among the dregs are a die, a button, and a coin.
I think I'll string them on a charm bracelet.

The raging voice of reason cautions me.
Nonetheless, I take a perilous turn inwards
to tend to my temple.
I tiptoe through the debris and remnants of a life not fully lived,
keeping bits I should have thrown,
tossing those I should have kept.
But who's to know when there's no peephole to the future.
No wonder one clings to the stains on the tablecloth or the tear
in a sheet.
It takes courage to walk away in search of the missing socks.

A butterfly alights on the windowpane,
its patchy wings all in a frenzy.
I stare at it rudely
for far too long.
But when it finally takes flight
I'm able to move on.

ASCENSION

I enter the forest under a milky sky with a layer of froth,
treading softly across its dank, dewy floor.
I wince at the shredded remains of a bird sowed among
the bleached bones of driftwood.
what new life will spring from this pyre?

I hurry on ahead until I catch up with the swaggering pines,
thick with sap,
a batch of candles with wax dripping down their sides.
I press my finger into the resin and put it to my mouth,
my tongue sizzling.
Only then do I spy the scaly skinned pinecones
hanging from the branches,
ready to bolt.

I come to a stream, gushing with gladness.
And I swoon before visions
of washer women clustered on a riverbank,
water bearers with pretty arched necks.
Then I spot the pinecones swimming downstream.
When they reach the ocean,
I think they will become fish.

I leave my fraternity of females
and travel to the fringe of the mountain,
its unshaven beard bristling with stubble.
I search for grace in its manliness.
For all my loveliness is there not a manliness in me?
Yesterday I was in love with the mountains.
Today they are cold and dark.
Tomorrow I will be in love with them again.

When I reach the peak I sit,
melting into the muffled silence.
I understand the hermit.
Above me the boughs of the pines are turned upward
like open palms
holding the faith for those below.
I have come to the place
where men and women are equal,
and fish and pinecones are one and the same.

THE FALLOW FIELDS

Doesn't the moodiness of late summer
remind you of a tired child,
all played out
but wanting one more go?

I would give in if I could,
a few more days of mirth and merrymaking,
granting the daisies a second bloom,
borrowing from the moon to give to the sun.
What difference would it make?
But it's not up to me.

So I will accept the meddling shadows,
dimming the light,
the parched grass
that's lost its springy step.
Tuckered out, it lays down for a long nap.

Soon the fields will lie fallow
and I will walk them,
back and forth,
keeping step with their weakening heartbeat,
priming my patience, honing my trust
for the long wait.

All winter I will tend the fields,
meticulously minding the maze,
cultivating emptiness,
storing it in my bowls.

Farewell to my summer friends,
the crickets, and ants, the ladybugs, the birds.
Each crisp night signals another departure.
Goodbyes are blistering.

The leaves flinch before turning their backs to me.
But I am not offended.

I eye the burnished bulbs
buried in a vase.
And a scrap of my spirit hunkers down with them.

I smile to think of the flurry when Winter turns over
and finds Spring in its bed.
There's bound to be a few days of seduction,
when energy rises and passions rule.
But Winter will retreat.

The currents of Spring will find their way back to me,
there will be a quickening in my fallow fields,
and I will fill my bowls of nothing.

Devotion

Everyone asks about the house next door,
wooden, with gingerbread trim,
and a broad smiling window
facing the sea.
It's an architectural wonder,
prepackaged, preordained,
sent all the way from Norway
at the turn of the century.

But no one asks who lived there.
Her name was Marie Magdalene Ourcival
and she was devoted,
constant in her care of her husband
who'd had the life knocked out of him at sixty-five,
bedbound for twelve years.

She was heedful of the white winged butterflies
that arrived each spring,
the thick ropes of honeysuckle
wrapped round rusty railings,
the comings and goings of the lark and the merlin,
even the crow who pillaged
the seeds she'd sewn.
She knew the name of every tiny thing
that inhabited her garden,
wild or otherwise.

She was devoted to her easel,
watercolor paintings of dawn,
embers of a passing night.

She had a bowl where she kept
stones that she'd gathered from the beach.
A butterfly collection hung from her bedroom wall.
An upstairs window was always open
gracing us with evening song.
Occasionally I caught the smell of a Sunday roast.
She lived to be one hundred and one.

After she died I climbed the stone steps of her garden,
chipped and warm,
and swam through the wiry vines,
pushing aside their sturdy stalks,
the rosemary bush,
the forbidden grapes,
all overgrown.
A blanket was folded over the back of her wicker chair,
a pitcher of water still on the table.
She was gone,
but I couldn't shed the feeling
that she lived and breathed
amidst all of this,
devoted in life
devoted in death.

TRESPASSERS

I take a strange delight in trespassers.
I don't mean the villains of news clips and films
who enter unbidden, poaching,
plundering property.

I'm talking about the neighboring cat that swivels along the
stone wall
and drops into the rose bed,
stopping to nudge the prickly pear,
rubbing her scruff against its burry neck.

There's the broad backed toad,
who incarnates at dusk,
barring the walkway with its cumbrous girth
and big-hearted croak.

Just the other night I had a visitor,
a gecko.
I'd shut the windows and locked the doors.
But somewhere, somehow,
when the house stretched and settled,
the lizard slipped in.

There it was, flattened against the bedroom ceiling,
next to a water stain from last month's rain
that trickled in under the eaves,
no regard for boundaries,
staring me in the face,
until at last, I said, "It's not your fault."

I watched the lizard for the longest time,
dipping into trance until I felt weightless.
It didn't move, not even a hair's breadth.
And I fell back asleep.
In the morning it was gone.

I went outside in search of it.
But my scouting was disturbed by the arrival of a crow.

She strutted across the stone tiles, then turned the turf,
a fortune hunter looking for buried treasure,
reminding me that I am the trespasser,
this place, only mine by deed.

Did you know that crows never forget a face?

SIGHTSEEING

This morning I saw an old woman
cocooned in a husky woolen coat and hat.
She looked like a question mark,
stooped, with black booted feet.

She shuffled towards me,
her masked face tilted towards the tuffets of grass
pinched painfully between the grooves of the sidewalk.
And I asked myself,
how could the cold have seeped so deeply into her bones
that her body could no longer perceive
the warm vapors of Spring
rising from the pavement?
How many winters had burned the fire
down to a patch of fleecy embers?

Recklessly, I lent her my eyes so that she could see all that I saw,
a painter with an easel and supplies tethered to his back.
He was heading towards the beach to capture
the breathtaking grip of the morning tide
clutching the shore.

I saw a white winged butterfly cartwheel across a lawn
and purple irises shimmying up a slope,
a color so rich and deep that I wanted to steal it.

There was someone lugging a foldable canvas chair,
straw yellow with stout wooden legs.
I watched him unpleat it and plant it in the sand,
among a crop of parasols
sprouting from the dunes.

A bicycle and a scooter whizzed by me
in a hurry to get on with the day and catch its glory
before it got away
as days do.

When I passed the olive-green flower truck,
giddy with tulips and puckered poppies,
I wanted to hop in and drive off.

All of this I saw above my mask
and I felt wildly alive.

When the old woman reached me, she lifted her head.
We couldn't have a conversation through our muffled masks.
Nor could I take the hand fluttering on her cane.
But I could look back at her, straight in the eyes,
And that was enough to stoke the fire.

THIS CHANGING WORLD

We're driving up to the highway,
the one that burrows right through
the mountains,
fuzzy now with winter fluff.
They're moving,
or maybe it's the clouds.

A string of thoughts snags my brain,
like how remarkable it is that
the mountains barely flinch
when the heavy machinery
bores a hole through their belly,
or rips a road up their sides.

I still don't see how the trees,
the dwellings,
rooted to the rim,
don't topple and fall.

How is it that the mountains sleep
through this racket and rumpus?
How kind they are, how generous,
at least for now.

But I know better.
Last year during a rainstorm
the mountains spit boulders
that bounced down the sides of the mountain,
gaining speed,
prying turf loose,
felling trees.

They landed on the highway,
mangling metal.
And my perfect world
of sandcastles and mudpies was
demolished.

I don't trust the mountains like I used to.
And I know it's just a question of time
before they roll over in their sleep
and rise again.

Come One, Come All

Come one, come all,
come into my home.
Leave your shoes at the door.
Be calm and enter.

Sit down at my table and help yourself to some grapes.
I plucked them from the vines this morning.
Or have a peach, or an apricot.
There's bread and cheese,
and olive paste,
if you'd rather.

I will pour you a drink.
Iced coffee or tea, or perhaps a prosecco,
or even a beer.
There's nothing better than a cool glass of water.

Speak to me of all and of nothing,
and don't be surprised if the cat chimes in.
She's always got something to say.

I can share a thing or two about growing older,
when the body becomes a burden
and the soul begins to speak.
It may sound like I'm talking in tongues,
but one day you'll understand me.

Just look at the cobweb that the crystal lamp casts upon the wall
next to a shimmering sunspot,
hieroglyphics of a higher consciousness,
no doubt.

Cross the floor and listen to the ache of the wooden planks,
the rustle of water swooshing through the pipes.
The wind in the attic is turning over in its sleep.

Reach into a nook or a cranny
of which there are many.
But beware of the ghosts of past, present, future.

Step into the room next door.
The chairs are waiting, arms spread wide.
Strike the piano keys and hear the sound linger
like the farewell of a friend.
Or turn the crank of the music box.
Don't be shy to sing along.

There's a basket of yarn beside the table.
Knit something if you'd like.
The travelling, back and forth,
will take you somewhere.
I promise.

Follow me up the winding staircase.
No need to hurry.
Take care of the wobbly wooden rail on iron legs.
It's been a long day.

Try not to frown at the chips in the wainscoting,
or the blemishes on the wall.
They are signs of a life well-lived.

Go straight to the green room and bask in the coolness
seeping from the walls.
Peek into the dollhouse,
and wish you could step into the miniature boots
and walk down the tiny hallway.

There's a bookcase in the red room,
right next to the bed.
Scan the shelves and take a volume.
Of course, you may borrow it.

There's a tiger in the blue room,
guarding the gate.
But don't worry.
It's not real.

Stretch your arms and feel the joy of children
who have shed the skins of youth
around the house.
They are all grown up now.

Throw open a window,
and gaze across the rooftops,
all the way to the sea.
I am almost certain that beyond is dreamland.

Stay for dinner
and we'll build a fire
and sit around
sinking nimbly into the night
in soulful companionship.

Come one, come all.
Come into my home.

4

CONTEMPLATING COSMOS

WHEATGRASS

I find the wind jolly,
even when it sneaks in like rogue waves,
fistfuls of might,
pummeling the wheatgrass,
sending their spindly stalks into convulsions.
I catch hold of a spear or two,
hoping to steal a moment of their happiness
before it's blown away.
That's the idea anyway.

I don't mind that their feathery heads are unkempt,
that each moves differently.
After all, no one thing is like another.

I am not concerned about leaving this earthly plane.
It's coming back that troubles me.
I know I will be offered a new body,
a human form.
But what if I'd rather be a stalk of wheatgrass?
That way of life would suit me,
anchored to the soil in a delicious bed of pine needles, dried
leaves, and stone chips,
sprouting out of the ground's coarse belly,
bending to its imperceptible pulse,
nourished in a way I never was.

How much simpler life would be.
Oh, I know life would be short,
but death is certain,
and dying close to the earth is the only way to go.

LIVING IN THE MARGINS

I have a brother,
first born,
first shoot on the family tree,
plumped with promise,
fed by expectation.
He lives in the margins,
the hinterland of exiled words, odd punctuation marks,
an array of misfits, so to speak,
usually of another color or cast
that don't fit the narrative on the page.

He was searching for a way out of a darkness,
so unbearable that his eyes never grew accustomed to it,
a deep discomfort,
the constant, pinching ache of ill ease.

Burnout,
burn black,
burn crazy.

So he reached for a bottle,
and one morning found himself tottering on the curb.
Then he stumbled over a comma or left out a full-stop
in the chronicle of his own life.
And he tumbled into the margins,
nudged by despair,
when life showed him what it was all about,
that love can be cutting,
loss can be cruel.

He is no longer one of us.
He is one of them.
Occasionally he steps back onto the page for a visit.
But we know he will never return.
He has set up home there among the lawless,
among his own kind,
deviants, mavericks, lost souls,
free of the constraints of grammatical rules.
A force greater than gravity,
called belonging,
keeps him there.

Once upon a time I shunned the margins,
home to humiliation and shame.
But then a tiny voice told me
that somewhere in the margins,
through an alchemy of broken souls,
is the gold of human existence.

THE ECSTASY OF TREETOPS

Over the arched bridge,
its stone spine weathering the drub of footsteps
all day long,
just on the other side of the river,
where the mallard ducks bleat and caw,
spinning in interminable circles—
it's enough to make the sun dizzy—
there's a tidy row of olive trees.
They swagger and sway seductively,
a chorus line,
reminding me that once,
many moons ago,
I, too, was in a dance troop.
We shimmied and shuffled and did the can-can,
arms linked paper-doll like.
But those olive trees know things I don't.
They've seen things I haven't.
They persist in their gyrations,
rousing the pines, the wooly headed hemlocks,
the sycamores with their vitiligo trunks.
And I'm left to wonder
is this how to get closer to God.

To Be a Star

Those nights, warm as wonder,
sticky as sap on the pines
that hover over terra cotta tiled roofs,
I wake,
mummified in my sheets,
unable to sleep.

I go outside and tilt my chin to the sky,
black as bean soup,
pitted with throbbing stars,
thousands of light years away.

I've thought about the life of a star,
probably too much if truth be told.
I'm charmed by their tiny, dazzling faces.
And if I look long enough,
I feel an insufferable want
stirring inside of me.

That's when I imagine a beam,
a glowing lifeline.
And I hoist myself into the heavens.

I wade through galaxies,
serenading the stars,
listening to their stories, their secrets.
I meet the bears, the lions, the hunter, that roam their world.

I study their motions and make them mine,
all with a singular purpose,
to come out at night,

disable darkness,
take possession,
and fill the void.

JUST A SCRIBE

I see it in their crestfallen faces
when they ask me where I get ideas for stories.
And I say, "from the ether."
They think I'm talking about chemistry, anesthetics,
all that's material.
But what I really mean is otherworldly,
the realms of spirit and air.

I say I'm just a scribe.
And that's a letdown too.
But it's true.
I'm writing down what reaches me,
from somewhere high up in the celestial soup.

I'm not afraid of those heights,
not like when I stand atop the Empire State building
clutched in a dizzying vortex,
stomach churning, knots galore.
Those heights are good and gracious,
home to all of creation.
I'm sure of that.

I don't mind being a scribe,
the fertile field for seeds
that enter me through invisible portals,
take root and then grow.
I write them down diligently.
And I can't help but think
that in this blessed world
there is no better task.

WOLF MOON

"Tonight there's a Wolf Moon," I say.
He doesn't care.
To him a full moon is
a hole punched in the sky,
a bucket of bright light.
To me it's a chance.

"The wolves are going to howl," I say.
"Let's see," he answers.

I spend the day
scraping the greyness from the livid sky
with nothing but my will.
Late afternoon the sky clears,
sax-blue with a tattering of clouds.

A train passes,
clickety-clack over the hot rolled steel rails,
beneath the wild purple irises that I hold precious,
like this Wolf Moon,
where I'll sew seeds of
courage and choice.

I step outside to meet evenfall.
He's standing behind me,
looking over my shoulder,
when the moon appears on the horizon,
bathed in orange, bursting bright.

"Wow," he says.
"That's a beauty."

"Can you hear the wolves?" I say.

"No," he answers.

"If you have ears, you can hear the voice of God," I say.
He'd told me that once.

"I hear the wolves," I say.

"And I hear the voice of God."

CLOUDS

Clouds are dear to me,
as are trees,
mud puddles,
and the cheesy paper moons
that cradle my loved ones in the photos on the mantle.
These things nourish me.

I don't think it's wasteful to watch a cloud cross the sky,
bask in the shade of a willow tree,
stomp in a puddle with shoeless feet.

Once I built a stone wall
with my own hands in the cleft of a hillside.
My nimble fingers pressed the stones into the tender turf,
one next to the other,
sealing them with sap and sludge
made from pools left by the rain.

The clouds saw me.
So did the trees.
And I'm sure that from somewhere,
on beyond,
my loved ones peered through the ether
and saw me too.
And it made me feel like I belonged.

From Where I Sit

From where I sit,
which is really all I want to do right now,
I can see the ocean through the branches of the orange tree.
They have a habit of diverging,
like wishbones.
And I have a habit of making wishes.
The ocean is only a sliver, slate-colored,
with white hyphens etched across a popply surface.
And it's moving to the right.
I think it's carrying away summer.

The bleached blue sky is propped above,
sitting there,
unmoving,
like me.
All around the trees are changing,
leaves turning in a torturous tango,
hanging lifeless from a thread.
Soon they will fall into their autumn beds.

I loved summer when it was here.
Its departure saddens me.
Goodbyes do that.

It's an in between time if you know what I mean.
Not dark, not light,
not hot, nor cold.
but something somewhere in the middle.

A few weeks back
a man did a painting of my house.

He thought he'd caught summer in his brush and splayed it
across his canvas.
But you can't catch summer,
or death for that matter.

But summer will return, as it always does.
And it will know where to find me.
I will be riding the waves,
coaxing the buttercups up a hill,
or just sitting in the wishbone limbs of the orange tree
watching and wishing.

Shoring Up

It's time to put away the wicker chairs,
bury the bulbs,
hang the lavender and thyme to dry.

The dull cast of the winter sky is hauntingly bright,
the smell of the turf like cedar dust.
I think I will lay low and listen to the earth's musings.

I'm ready to enter the unknown,
to be honest with myself and the land,
to clear the cabinets of body and soul.
It's time to die to another year.

Light the fires.
Feed the flames.
Give a book to a friend.

It's time to unite in readiness.
for the cold cruelness that lies ahead.

5

INTO THE ETHER

GRIEF

It came to me in a dream,
on the cusp of a mid-March moon,
from the astral plane where each detail of life
is meticulously catalogued,
a vision of loss clothed in a knowing so real it rattled my bones,
bleeding through my conscious,
burning a hole,
a blot on the movie screen of my life.

Then it happened.
My father died.
He left, and the visitors came in waves.
Amazing, isn't it, how past, present, and future
huddle haplessly around death?

The visitors parted slowly,
leaving an inky trail at the door.
Their odor, their clothes, their breath
became the smell of grief.
It set up in my house and stayed for many moons,
drifting through my body shamelessly,
a wayward traveler,
artfully dimming the light.

It beguiled me with its easy, nimble, ways.
its damp downy fuzz,
prickling the surface of my skin,
needling its way into my pores.
Its taste, damp and salty,
became a permanent fixture
on the tip of my tongue.

It brazenly climbed into my bed,
entwined itself in the sheets,
keeping me awake at night,
until one day I caught it pilfering,
leaching seeds of joy from my belly.
It tried to elude me with its sleight of hand tactics,
but I finally cornered it behind a kneecap, hard and taut.

I wrestled it to the ground,
determined to fight it to the death.
Then I chased it from my door.
But it slunk back, begging for attention.

I took pity on grief and let it back in.
I embraced it, stripped off its many layers,
right down to the marrow,
jellylike, with wobbling edges.
When I cleared away the roughage,
I tried to put it through a sieve.
But I couldn't separate the dregs from the beauty
until I got below its bubbling vapors.
Beneath was a shimmering pool,
deep blue,
a stillness at its center.
And, finally, I saw that I was grieving not only for what I lost,
but for what I never had.

What He did To Me

That guy pulled out of his pocket
a Saturday Night Special,
a cheap, slick, black barreled gun.
And he shot my father smack in the face.
The bullet exited the back of my father's head,
but it didn't stop there.
It travelled up the rocky coast,
swiveling past all the places my father loved,
leaving a bloodbath of bleeding hearts in its wake.

It gutted my family,
splitting our lives into before and after,
like neatly parted hair.

I lost my bearings as anyone might.
But it wasn't only that.
I lost my god.

My father didn't believe in God.
Nor did I.
But after my father left,
that changed.

I looked for God in all the wrong places.
How was I to know?
I was young and green.
I knew nothing beyond what my fingertips could touch.

When we finally met, years later,
I was walking a tightrope between life and death.
I'd momentarily stepped out of this world

to peer into another.
The encounter was brief,
but afterwards, I began to see God everywhere,
in my neighbor's smoking chimney,
the crackle of melting frost,
the twist of a climbing vine,
the leap of a cat.
I saw God in every person who passed.
That's what that guy did to me.
And I ought to be grateful

THE AFTERLIFE

Once I slipped into the ether.
It was an accident.
It happened as I lay on a cold metal plate,
a harsh light boring through my matrix of skin and bones.
I was locked in a deep sleep,
induced by sodium pentothal.

Body began to tremble,
quivering on the edge of nothingness.
Then it lost its grip and I slipped into the ether,
bridging both worlds.

Time and space double crossed me.
And I began to shrink as I floated upward.

I hoped to alight on an angel wing,
or a heavenly bed.
But, weightless, I floated through a stream of liquid light,
scooped up in a torrent of cross beams.
Then my eyes grew wide as saucers.
A lady in white drifted towards me,
beguiling me with her beauty.
"Take me with you," I cried, bounding towards her.
But she stopped me.
"You must go back," she said.
But I didn't want to return to the peril and pain
of my earthly existence.
So I broke.
I could hear the chink of my soul shattering.
My tears dripped into the streams of liquid light.
Then the lady in white drew nearer to me.

She pieced my parts together to make me whole.
She blessed me with her grace,
and the lights flashed off.
Next thing I knew I awakened on the cold metal table,
drugged, drowsy, trembling,
not from pain,
but from my taste of the afterlife.

THE PLACE OF BODY SELECTION

I knew what I was getting into
when I chose this Body.
I stood there,
naked soul,
in the place of body selection,
in the boundless light of eternity,
propped up by a clear-eyed, grey-haired guide named Aloicious.
He reminded me of a figure that I'd crossed
at the outdoor market
countless times.

I was drawn to this Body,
its lithe, supple form,
long, able fingers
made for casting and creation.
The other choices, five, in all,
dense as dogwood,
mouths open, eyes closed,
weren't right for the life I intended.

Aloicious warned me.
This Body was sensitive,
easily touched,
often wounded.
It would challenge me.
I would have to bear the salty sores of survival
over and over again.

I knew all of that.
But I didn't care.

This Body, tempered by hardship,
bone tired, broken.
I tend to it the best I can.
No matter that its faltering,
it's life force dimming.
This Body has served me well.
And I'm not going to whinge.

Maybe you think the notion of a place of body selection is
absurd,
laughable.
But I've been there.
Trust me.
It's as real as a penny in a pocket.

And if you like, I can charm you into a trance,
summon your soul,
and carry you into the ether,
where you, too, can alight at the place of body selection,
and discover why you
chose your body,
the temple of your being,
as home.

LEMONS AND LEAVES

I watched it happen to the lemon tree,
day after day,
when I took the stone path
that led right to my front door.
It was the tree that had filled my larder,
seasoned my soul with its bitter balm,
and flecks of sunshine from the peel.

Well, now there are no more lemons,
only leaves pinned loosely to bony branches.
At first there were dozens of them
acrobatic aces,
spryly twisting and turning.
But each day there are fewer.
Yesterday there were eight,
today, one.

And under the tree,
an amber skirting
where they've come to rest.
Who tells the leaves to change color,
to let go,
the branches to stiffen and grow homely nubs?
I like to think I'm like that tree.

I know that one day I'll enter
the winter of my being.
But that doesn't stop me from asking
how many leaves
are left on my tree.

Rare Bird

I don't remember much about that day,
only that it was unseasonably mild,
sundrops scattering the pavement,
false spring, teasing my senses.

They told me that a rare bird
had come to nest in my body.
Its whereabouts and ways were an enigma.
No one knew much about this bird,
beyond that it moved stealthily,
cautiously feeding on flesh,
and it usually never left.

Maybe I ought to feel special to host such a prized creature.
They treat me that way,
so much attention to the habits of this curious bird.

I confess
that I, too, spend hours studying the species,
learning its language,
coaxing the rare bird to listen,
encouraging it to take flight.

For the moment we are cohabiting.
But the truth is
I am now a guest in my own home.
And I never know when this bird will rise up,
unaware that my demise is its demise.
I wonder if it even cares.
But I am a hoper
and I keep believing

that one day the rare bird will die.
And I, like the phoenix, will rise from the ashes
and reclaim my place in this body
and in this world.

INTO THE ETHER

Will it hurt, you ask,
when Body bellows its last few breaths and Soul stirs,
preparing to take leave of the dense moorings of skin and bone,
struggling to detach from the shreds of Body
that still cling to life,
the taut tether of earthly existence.

Once again that spiteful sting of separation.
Have you forgotten that you've done this again and again?
Perhaps death is not what you think.

Take heart.
The lingering soul is not yesterday's lover, slipping off at dawn,
or the setting sun, turning its back on day.
There is no haste, no harsh good-byes,
nothing, but a tender longing as Soul hovers over Body,
contemplating its wounds with tender regard,
casting a quiet dignity on the ache of ages.
The journey towards wisdom is long and hard.

It's a time of reckoning
as soul tends to the chores of packing up,
mapping memories, cataloging regrets,
words unsaid, deeds undone.

Speak heart
of your comings and goings,
a treasured child,
body's reward for the searing pain of birth
at the service of soul,
the death of a beloved.

There is a merging and melting of boundaries
as Soul bows before its temple to bid it goodbye.
"Thank you, Body."
And maybe, for the first time,
Body feels embraced by love.

Then Body is cast off gently,
an item of well-worn clothing, soiled and scarred,
and Soul leaves home, closing the door.

At last Body is free to begin its own exodus,
and Soul left to lift its wings and fly into the ether,
homeward bound.

It's good to be home where Soul
meets Self
and finally is told, "You did well."

PRACTICING DEATH

I understand the impossibility of death
in the net of aliveness that holds us captive,
the hubbub of life that kindles our senses.
Who isn't struck by the daffodils,
newborn babes,
poking their heads above ground,
catching their first breath?

It's hard to believe that death, too, is alive,
but I know better.
I'm familiar with its pitiful pranks,
plotted to garner our attention,
like hummingbirds,
pecking away.

All I ask is to meet death gracefully,
fall into its arms with the same ardor I embrace life.
Waking lotus,
dying lily.

After all every day is a death,
each season,
each lapse into sleep,
those awkward endings for the poet and bard.
Why not let go of the bounty
and savor the scanty moments of stillness?
Become friends with death
before its yours.
And know that it's another beginning.

BURN BABY BURN

Some days,
lately,
I dare to envisage myself
melting the material,
and crafting a new reality
from its molten molecules.

Burn, baby, burn.

Some nights,
lately,
I dream of dipping into the infinite pools of possibility.
I'm not afraid of
tumbling into eternity,
surrendering self.
I'll take that chance.

Imagine,
rising from the ashes,
sound and sane,
free of disease,
a new body,
a new life,
forged from the alchemy of Being.

I am not to say what is
or what isn't.
But don't make me walk over the coals
without believing there's more to life
than this dirt, fire, and air.

SAINTS AND MYSTICS

I like to read about saints,
Hildegarde of Bingen, Theresa of Lisieux, Mary Magdalene,
their lives of devotion,
how they tended their gardens and hearth,
their unbreakable faith,
their indifference to death.
I have grown accustomed to their vapors,
lingering in my space.
They move through my life like others,
infusing me with hope and strength.

You say it's an illusion,
crumpet crumbs for the hungry,
that I've created from dust and fancy.
But I won't give up the kind-hearted companionship,
the wise, loving counsel of these ethereal beings.

Do you know that Saint Hildegarde had a secret Alphabet?
No one has been able to crack the code,
not scholars, nor mystics.
I am neither.
But I have steeped myself in Hildegarde's aura
for long enough to know with conviction
that her Secret Alphabet
is her confessions.

FOOTSTEPS

Footsteps.
They follow me everywhere these days.
I hear them somewhere behind me, off in the distance,
a dim but constant, tap tap.
Can't you hear them?
Even while I sleep,
they tiptoe through my dreams.
And when I rise in the morning,
I hear their cadence,
alongside the chittering birds,
the banging of the garbage bins,
and the click clack of the blinders opening.

At times, the footsteps grow quicker, more hollow,
especially now that the days are shorter,
the fields flat,
trees brushed bare by the fall wind,
driftwood amassing on the beach,
shoring up for winter.
They echo in the emptiness of a dying season.

I've grown used to them.
I know that one day they will overtake me.
But I try not to let it bother me.

WHY I SAID NO

I said no to the drugs,
no to the rays that might keep me alive
for a few more months or so.
I couldn't do that to Body.

Maybe I wouldn't live forever.
But no one does.
Not here anyway.

But I could be kind to Body
for the time we had left.
I could wind my arms around my wasted frame,
or lay a palm on my bruised bones and burning skin.
I could say thank you for a life well lived.
After all Body had been my home for a long time.

But I couldn't poison my kidneys
or taint my marrow,
the vessels for what life force I had left,
the seat of my family.
I wouldn't burn the roots of my people or past.

Pain, well, that was an old friend.
A little more, a little less.
It was all right.

I would live for as long as I could
not just being me
which was, after all,
just a speck in the universe.
I would be a kinky branch on the orange tree,

a spider that hangs from the cord on the yellow blind,
a drop of water that leaks from the spout I never had fixed.

I would die whole,
no matter how frail and damaged I was.
And so I said,
no.

What do I Leave Them

How can I catch a corner of a cloud,
or a patch of blue sky,
the song of a sparrow,
the blink of a lizard,
or one of those stars that nosedive across the night sky curdling
my tummy?

I could press a leaf or a wildflower into
one of my favorite books,
or pilfer a feather or a tree pod
from the forest floor.

But the trouble is,
they perish,
and things that don't,
well, they're not worth it.

Sure, there are memories,
But they fade too.
And I'm left with the same dilemma.
How do I leave them a snippet
of the beauty and wonder I see
each time I look out at the world.

ACKNOWLEDGMENTS

I would like to acknowledge my earthy family, my spiritual family, and the inhabitants of the natural world, all of whom reflected back to me, in their own unique way, the images that have become my vision of the world. And I wish to honor the gracious gift that enabled me to put words to this vision and to share it. Thank you.